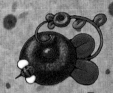

Ain't Life Grand!
a Treasury for Grandmothers

Illustrated by Mary Engelbreit

Andrews McMeel
Publishing, LLC

Kansas City

and Mary Engelbreit® are registered trademarks
of Mary Engelbreit Enterprises, Inc.

07 08 09 10 11 LEO 10 9 8 7 6 5 4 3

ISBN-13: 978-0-7407-6367-0
ISBN-10: 0-7407-6367-9

Library of Congress Control Number: 2006931421

Compiled by Patrick Regan

www.andrewsmcmeel.com
www.maryengelbreit.com

Ain't Life Grand!

a Treasury for Grandmothers

Being grandparents sufficiently removes us from the responsibilities so that we can be friends.

—Allan Frome

For my darling grandmothers,
Ann Estelle and Bess

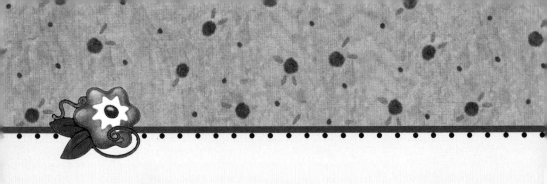

Contents

Introduction

Both of my grandfathers died before I was born, but my grandmothers lived until I was in my teens. Boy, did they live! Mine were not the stereotypical, folksy grandmothers of storybooks with aprons always on and silver hair done up in tidy buns. Both my grandmothers, who incidentally had been friends in girlhood, were vibrant, opinionated, funny, and sophisticated women. They had full lives, lots of friends, and—I remember this so well—really beautiful clothes.

I remember as a girl getting to go out to lunches with my mother, my aunt, and my mom's mother (who many readers know was the original Ann Estelle). My sister and I loved listening to the grown-up conversations, feeling privileged just to be a part of what I felt was such a glamorous and worldly group of women. They seemed not so much like a different generation as a different breed entirely. Ann Estelle was a true character—elegant and refined, but also a real flirt, and really cute. She raised my mother and aunt in the same mold, and those two generations had a lot in common. As for me, I'm not often accused of being glamorous, but I think that my grandmother's love of life and sense of humor has managed to trickle down.

My paternal grandmother was equally elegant but more hands-on with my sisters and me. She baby-sat us regularly and loved making a fuss over us. She would make us beautiful dresses and always brought us white gloves on Easter.

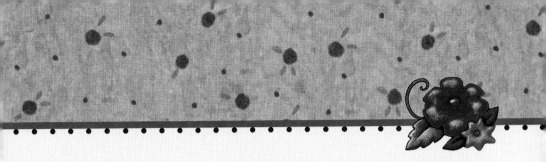

She would do our nails, which we thought was the most exotic thing in the world. I remember that she used to comb my hair and tell me that it was just like spun gold. (If that isn't a grandmotherly thing to say, I don't know what is.)

One by one, now, the little girls I grew up with are becoming grandmothers, too. Because we are still friends all these years later, we have the privilege of swapping grandchild stories just as we have shared so many things over the years. When I think of my own grandmothers now, they do seem to belong to a different age. After all, a grandmother today is just as likely to go on a ten-mile bike ride with her granddaughter as sew her a new outfit. But the essence of what my grandmothers passed along to me still holds value today. It was from their strong example that I learned to carry myself proudly, live every minute of life, believe in myself, and behave like a proper lady (most of the time, anyway). But perhaps more than anything else, what my grandmothers showed me was how to grow older gracefully. For that, I am eternally grateful.

I compiled this book as a tribute to grandmothers both new and "experienced." Families just wouldn't be complete without them.

Yours,

Mary

It is as grandmothers that our mothers come into the fullness of their grace.

—Christopher Morley

Perfect love sometimes does not come
until the first grandchild.

—Welsh Proverb

If nothing is going well,
call your grandmother.

—Italian Proverb

You do not really understand something
unless you can explain it
to your grandmother.

—Proverb

You've got to do your own growing,
no matter how tall
your grandfather was.

—Irish Proverb

13

Not many years ago,

I was in the middle of a busy morning. Sarah was tagging along, helping me around the house.

"What are you doin', Grandma?

"I'm straightening the living room. The girls are coming for bridge this afternoon."

"What girls, Grandma?" By now the kid was jumping on the couch.

"You know, Sarah. The girls I play bridge with on Wednesdays. My friends—"

"Yeah, yeah. I know!" she crowed. "You mean the girls with the grandmother faces."

Excerpt from *The Girls with the Grandmother Faces* by Frances Weaver, New York; Hyperion, 1996.

It's amazing how grandparents seem so young once you become one.

—Anonymous

Grandma Me

By Lois Wyse

Who can ever imagine the sense of grandmotherhood? Who can ever picture herself a rocking-chair granny?

Mommy, yes.

But grandmother? Certainly not I.

Like all grandparents, I was given a warning of some months about the event, but who can be prepared?

The first person to clue me in to the world of grandparenthood was my friend Isabelle. We were lunching, and somewhere between the salad and the coffee, I broke the news. Yes, I was very thrilled. Yes, I was ready. Yes, I understood what it would mean.

Isabelle listened and then sat back and smiled knowingly.

I was bewildered by her smugness.

"You only think you know," she said sagely. "Wait. Just wait. No matter what you expect, you won't be prepared."

She was right.

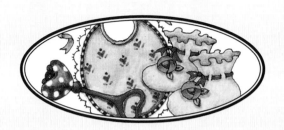

I wasn't prepared when the call came at 4 a.m. that the baby would be born within hours.

I rushed to the airport, caught a 7 a.m. plane, and ran for a cab to take me to the hospital. I did not telephone from the airport to learn what happened (I could not bear to hear about this birth from an impersonal voice on the telephone).

I went immediately to the maternity-floor waiting room, where all our family was assembled, and I heard those wonderful words. "It's a healthy girl born ten minutes ago."

So.

Ten minutes old and already this little girl was arriving ahead of me.

Moments later, in her father's arms, the baby came to meet us.

To my shock and amazement I burst into tears. But not just ordinary, run-of-the-mill tears. This was old-fashioned, heart-rending sobbing. For in that moment I was touched by every life that had preceded this new one.

My father, dead before even my son was born, was there. So, too, were my grandparents, great-grandparents, uncles, aunts, cousins. In a great, convulsive tide I was swept back to my beginnings—child, young wife, mother.

I was filled with the enormity of that sense of belonging, all of us, each to the other. We are bound by our own inexorable, nonending saga. We are the human story. We are us. And now she is us. And only God knows what lies ahead of us—and all life.

No wonder I cried inconsolably.

No wonder my friend could not describe it.

Appeared originally in *Good Housekeeping* magazine.

19

Grandma always made you feel
she had been waiting to see just you all day
and now the day was complete.

—Marcy DeMaree

20

What a bargain grandchildren are!
I give them my loose change,
and they give me a million dollars'
worth of pleasure.

—Gene Perret

They say genes skip generations.
Maybe that's why grandparents
find their grandchildren so likable.

—Joan McIntosh

When a Child Is Born, So Is a Grandmother

By Jan Miller Girando

A grandchild!
The news puts your life in a tizzy.
You've just been promoted!
You'd better get busy.

There's so much to shop for—
Time's zooming already!
Let's see: Little play suits,
A terrycloth teddy,
Bright alphabet blocks
And a juice cup in sterling—
In no time, the tiny tyke
Has your life whirling!

This gathering of goods
Is no open-and-shut case;
You've got to switch gears
Or turn into a nutcase!

Relax—take the load off!
Enjoy the transition.
Regain your mystique
And serene composition!

A grandma with flair
And a sense of direction,
You'll focus on style—
It's more fun than perfection!

You'll write your own rules
And you'll do your own thinking.
You'll grandparent your way!
Without even blinking,
You'll add to the pink and blue
World of the baby
Your own splash of color
(Or just a dash, maybe).

You're launching your legacy
With innovation
And boldly defining
The next generation!

No need to wear aprons,
Make pies, or bake cookies—
That timeworn scenario's
Strictly for rookies!

Select from the past
The traditions you treasure,
Then give them your own
Special flair for good measure

Who cares if your talent
For sewing or knitting
Is subpar at best?
Make your mark baby-sitting!
Read Mother Goose, Dr. Seuss,
Winnie-the-Pooh—
Tell tales of "the olden days"
Featuring you!

You're bound to excel
In advanced coochy-cooing;
Before long, you'll know
When the storm clouds are brewing!
If fussing transpires,
No need for a stand-off—
Find Mommy or Daddy
And relish the hand-off!

Adapt a demeanor
That's cool and collected.
When tantrums begin,
You remain unaffected.
If food becomes airborne
Or rooms get disheveled,
Just take a backseat
Till the discipline's leveled!

Let Mom and Dad handle
The scowling and scolding . . .
A grandma's around
For the hugging and holding,
For listening to secrets,
For teaching and sharing,
For offering a lifetime
Of comfort and caring.

A loyal supporter
Of every endeavor,
You'll share a close bond
With your grandchild forever.
A beautiful future's
Unfolding for you—
When a grandchild is born,
A grandmother is, too.

Becoming a grandmother is wonderful.
One moment you're just a mother.
The next you are all-wise and prehistoric.

—Pam Brown

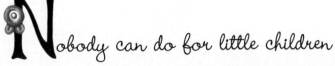

$\mathcal{N}$obody can do for little children
what grandparents do.
Grandparents sort of sprinkle stardust
over the lives of little children.

—Alex Haley

We should all have one person
who knows how to bless us
despite the evidence.
Grandmother was that person to me.

—Phyllis Theroux

A Truly Grand Day

The grandest of achievements really do begin with one committed person. In 1970, Marian Lucille Herndon McQuade, a West Virginia housewife, initiated a campaign to set aside a special day just for grandparents. Through her concerted efforts and with help from civic, business, church, and political leaders, the campaign expanded statewide. The first Grandparent's Day was proclaimed in 1973 in West Virginia by Governor Arch Moore.

In the same year, West Virginia Senator Jennings Randolph introduced a Grandparent's Day resolution in the U.S. Senate. After five years—and lots more campaigning by Mrs. Herndon McQuade—the U.S. Congress passed legislation proclaiming the first Sunday after Labor Day as National Grandparent's Day. The proclamation was signed by President Jimmy Carter. Today, the event begun by one devoted soul is observed by millions throughout the country. Way to go, Marian!

I n My Grandmother's House

By Bonnie Christensen

What makes us who we are? Education? Environment? Or is it family, the sticky web of who went before, past generations, or family trees? Young faces stare out from tintype photos. Who is she? Why doesn't anyone say a word about him? Family secrets. Skeletons rattling. All of it funnels down to each of us. Some material we accept and cherish. Some we reject or deny. But even what we choose to accept or deny is influenced by our families and family history.

My grandmother once owned a large vanity with two hinged side mirrors, which I often closed around myself to create a hall of endless reflections, echoing smaller and smaller in the distance. Though initially it seemed all the images emanated from the largest, closest reflection, the longer I stood there the more it seemed equally possible that it all began with the farthest, almost infinitely small figure. Or perhaps there was no definite beginning or end at all. All I knew for sure was that my focus fell on neither the largest reflection nor the smallest, but on a reflection just a few steps away from myself, in the same space occupied by my grandmother in the chain of our family. Close enough to be comfortable but enough removed to evoke mystery.

Perhaps the mystery of grandmothers is related to the past we never knew, including the inconceivable fact that our parents were once children—our grandmother's children. And, because grandmothers often don't live nearby, they're removed by the mysteries of both time and space. So how do they manage to seem comfortably close? Like the reflection in the mirror—not too near and not too far.

Excerpted from *In My Grandmother's House*: New York: Harper Collins Children's Books, 2003.

Uncles and aunts, and cousins,

are all very well,

and fathers and mothers are not to be despised;

but a grandmother, at holiday time,

is worth them all.

—Fanny Fern

A grandmother pretends she doesn't know who you are on Halloween.

—Erma Bombeck

$\mathcal{A}$ mother becomes a true grandmother
the day she stops noticing
the terrible things her children do
because she is so enchanted
with the wonderful things
her grandchildren do.

—Lois Wyse

When grandparents enter the door,
discipline flies
out the window.

—Ogden Nash

My grandmother started walking
five miles a day when she was sixty.
She's ninety-seven now,
and we don't know where the hell she is.

—Ellen DeGeneres

34

My grandmother is over eighty
   and still doesn't need glasses.
Drinks right out of the bottle.

—Henry Youngman

Have children while your parents
   are still young enough to take care of them.

—Rita Rudner

The Grannies

By Pat Cummings

Grandmotherwise, I've been lucky. I got the sensible-shoed, silver-haired, ample-bosomed, candy-jar-on-the-coffee-table women who worked hard and made clear their devotion to their families. They both wore dresses at home! Fried food! Kept ladylike gloves in their top dresser drawer! They even filled pantries with cans and boxes whose contents could be whipped into dinners for six. I saw them do it. And, most importantly, they doled out the kind of unconditional love that, to this day, buffers me against any slings and arrows in my path.

I suspect grandmothers will always be wells of unconditional love, always be fonts of wisdom and guardians of tradition. Some things never change. A lot of my memories of my grandmothers involve food, however, so I'm glad I got the cookie-baking, deep-frying, snack-friendly treatment from them before everyone got so nervous about sugar and cholesterol. Being indulged senseless was a big part of being a grandchild when I was little.

So here's what I've decided happens: Eventually, with a bit of luck, you reach your grandmother's age. You look in the mirror and you see the spot you saw on her face, or the line at the corner of your mouth that is just like hers. And, sure enough, whenever I study

their photos now, I'm starting to see myself. As late as it is, which is too late, I find myself wishing that these women whom I so clearly came from had had the gentler life they helped me have. That desire, retroactive and pointless, leaves a dull, radiating ache in my chest whenever I let my mind go down that path. I can't indulge them, now that I finally understand that they may have enjoyed a bit of indulgence. I can't lavish on them what they lavished on others. They gave a lot. I took a lot. Some things they handed over, some things I inherited. And some things seeped in just from being in the room while they talked.

I sometimes feel my grandmothers with me still. Occasionally in dreams. Oddly enough, in patches of sunlight. In memories that spring up while I'm sitting at my drawing table or walking down a tree-lined street. I have no idea why these memories come when they do. And certainly, a whiff of any dish either one of them used to cook can propel me right back to their kitchens in Chicago. Diet gurus might preach that my Pavlovian buttons need to be disconnected—but disconnect the aroma of macaroni and cheese, biscuits and pies, and potato salad?

Excerpted from *In My Grandmother's House* by Bonnie Christensen, New York: Harper Collins Children's Books, 2003.

THE COMFORTER

Our grandchildren accept us for ourselves,

without rebuke or effort to change us,

as no one in our entire lives has ever done,

not our parents, siblings, spouses, friends—

and hardly ever our own grown children.

—Ruth Goode

The simplest toy,
one which even the youngest child
can operate,
is called a grandparent.

—Sam Levenson

Few things are more delightful
than grandchildren fighting over your lap.

—Doug Larson

$\mathcal{I}$f becoming a grandmother
was only a matter of choice,
$\mathcal{I}$ should advise every one of you straight
away to become one.
There is no fun for old people like it!

—Hannah Whithall Smith

GLAM GRAM

harms for the Easy Life

By Kaye Gibbons

Already by her twentieth birthday, my grandmother was an
excellent midwife, in great demand. Her black bag bulged with mysteries in vials. This occupation led her to my grandfather, whose job
was operating a rope-and-barge ferry that traveled across the
Pasquotank River. A heavy cable ran from shore to shore, and he
pulled the cable and thus the barge carrying people, animals, every-
thing in the world, across the river. My grandmother was a frequent
passenger, going back and forth over the river to catch babies, nurse
the sick, and care for the dead as well. I hear him singing as he pulls
her barge. At first it may have annoyed her, but soon it was a sound
she couldn't live without. She may have made up reasons to cross the
river so she could hear him and see him. Think of a man content
enough with quiet nights to work a river alone. Think of a man content to bathe in a river and drink from it, too. As for what he saw
when he looked at my grandmother, if she looked anything like my
mother's high school graduation photograph, she was dazzling, her
green eyes glancing from his to the water to the shore. Between my
grandmother, her green eyes and mound of black hair, and the big-
cookie moon low over the Pasquotank, it must have been all my
grandfather could do to deposit her on the other side of the river.

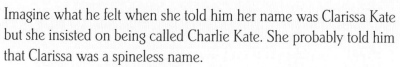

Imagine what he felt when she told him her name was Clarissa Kate but she insisted on being called Charlie Kate. She probably told him that Clarissa was a spineless name.

Now, some facts of her life I have not had to half invent by dream. She and my grandfather were married by a circuit rider in 1902 and lived in a tiny cabin on the Pasquotank, completely cut off from everybody but each other. My grandmother continued to nurse people who lived across the river, and soon Indian women in the vicinity came to prefer her root cures to their own. My mother was born here in 1904. She was delivered by an old Indian woman named Sophia Snow, thus her name, Sophia Snow Birch. My grandmother became hung in one of those long, deadly labors common to women of the last century. After thirty-six hours of work with little result, my grandmother decided she would labor standing, holding on to the bedpost for support, letting gravity do what it would. Sophia, however, persuaded her to be quilled, and so a measure of red pepper was blown up my grandmother's nose through the end of a feather freshly plucked from one of her many peacocks. My grandmother fell into a sneezing frenzy, and when she recovered enough to slap Sophia, she did. Sophia slapped her back, earning both my grandmother's respect and an extra dollar. Within the hour, my mother was born.

Excerpt from *Charms for the Easy Life*, New York; Putnam, 1993.

$\mathcal{E}$veryone needs to have access
both to grandparents and grandchildren
in order to be
a full human being.

—Margaret Mead

$\mathbf{I}$f your baby is
"beautiful and perfect,
never cries or fusses,
sleeps on schedule
and burps on demand,
an angel all the time,"
you're the grandma.

—Teresa Bloomingdale

Most grandmas have of touch of the scallywag.

—Helen Thomson

What children need most are the essentials
that grandparents provide in abundance.
They give unconditional love, kindness,
patience, humor, comfort, lessons in life.
And, most importantly, cookies.

—Rudolph Giuliani

49

My Grandmother's Hands

By Arlene "Callie" Hills

The cloth-folding fingers that snip at the thread
Seem blessed by dexterity I thought long dead
Are these skills my own, or directed by one
Whose hands never rested 'til her years were done?

Grandmother's hands, grandmother's hands,
Am I being guided by grandmother's hands?
Grandmother's hands, grandmother's hands,
Perhaps I am guided by grandmother's hands.

I sit in my sewing room night after night
Sometimes from sunset 'til early dawn light
With costumes and fabrics too many to name
Each project unique but the patience the same.

Her slim, nimble fingers were ever employed
Creating great beauty that many enjoyed
For family and friends, Nile or Eastern Star
She knit, baked, or cross-stitched from daylight 'til dark.

Her legacy lives in her family's minds
Some sew and some bake and some others draw lines
With cinnamon rolls, flowers, or hairpin lace,
Each item an offering of talent and grace

Grandmother's hands, grandmother's hands,
Perhaps we are guided by grandmother's hands,
Grandmother's hands, grandmother's hands,
I think we're all guided by grandmother's hands.

Grandchildren are God's way
of compensating us
for growing old.

—Mary H. Waldrip

52

Elephants and grandchildren never forget.

—Andy Rooney

What is it about grandparents that is so lovely?
I'd like to say that grandparents
              are God's gifts to children.
And if they can but see,
hear, and feel what these people have to give,
       they can mature at a fast rate.

—Bill Cosby

53

Grandmothers Are to Love

By Lois Wyse

Here are some words
About somebody big
Who loves somebody little . . .

Oh, there are a lot of people
Who love you . . .

The bakery lady
Who gives you a cookie,
Your uncle in Oskaloosa,
The next-door neighbor with bangs
Loves you
And so does
The dog across the street.

There are two second cousins
Who love you,
And your teacher
Thinks you are a dear.
The policeman, the mailman,
And the bus driver love you.

And . . . oh yes . . .
So do your mother and father.

But this somebody who loves you
Looks a little like a mother,
Smiles a lot like a father,
And has two pictures of you
In her purse.

This somebody who loves you
Makes good thick soup
And good thin cookies
And brings you sand from Florida.

This somebody who loves you
Takes you out to lunch
And invites you over to sleep.

This somebody who loves you
Shortens your clothes
And raised your parents.

This somebody who loves you
Dries your tears,
Tells you stories,
And shows you which one
Is the petunia.

This somebody who loves you
Holds your hand
When you hop the puddles,
Holds you tight
When you feel sad,
And holds you up
To see the parade.

This somebody who loves you is called
Mimi
Nana
Bubby
Noo-noo
Gamma
Gaga
Granny
Or Grandma

But no matter what you call her,
She's your grandmother.

And if you have a grandmother,
Aren't you a lucky one?
For grandmamas do many things
So grandbabies have fun.

When parents go away
Grandmamas do the sitting,

And if you need warm mittens,
Granny tends to the knitting.

If you have some clothes
That you call your Sunday best,
Chances are it's Nana's gift
That makes you so well-dressed.

But the gifts of clothes and seashells
That grandmothers think of
Mean nothing next to your gift,
The priceless gift of love.

For the most valued jewel of Grandma's
Is not diamond or topaz,
But the precious little child
That her child now has.

You've a very special trust.
Remember this . . . please do,
The love of generations
Is handed down to you.

So if you have a grandma
Thank the Good Lord up above,
And give Grandmama hugs and kisses,
For grandmothers are to love.

If you want to civilize a man,
begin with his grandmother.

—Victor Hugo

Being pretty on the inside
means you don't hit your brother
and you eat all your peas—
that's what my grandma taught me.
—Lord Chesterfield

The closest friends
I have made all through life
have been people
who also grew up close
to a loved and living
grandmother or grandfather.
—Margaret Mead

 house needs a grandma in it.

—Louisa May Alcott

Acknowledgments

Andrews McMeel Publishing has made every effort to contact the copyright holders.

Page 14: Excerpted from *The Girls with the Grandmother Faces* by Frances Weaver. Copyright © 1996 Frances Weaver. Reprinted by permission of Hyperion. All rights reserved.

Page 30: Excerpted from *In My Grandmother's House* by Bonnie Christensen copyright © 2003 by Bonnie Christensen. Published by Harper Collins Childrens Books. All right reserved. Used with permission.

Page 36: From "The Grannies" by Pat Cummings copyright © 2003 by Pat Cummings. Reprinted by permission of the author.

Page 44: From *Charms for the Easy Life* by Kaye Gibbons, copyright © 1993 by Kaye Gibbons. Used by permission of G.P. Putnam's Sons, a division of Penguin Group (USA) Inc.

Page 50: "My Grandmother's Hands" by Arlene "Callie" Hills. Lyrics copyright © 1997 by Arlene "Callie" Hills. Reprinted by permission of the author.

Illustrations